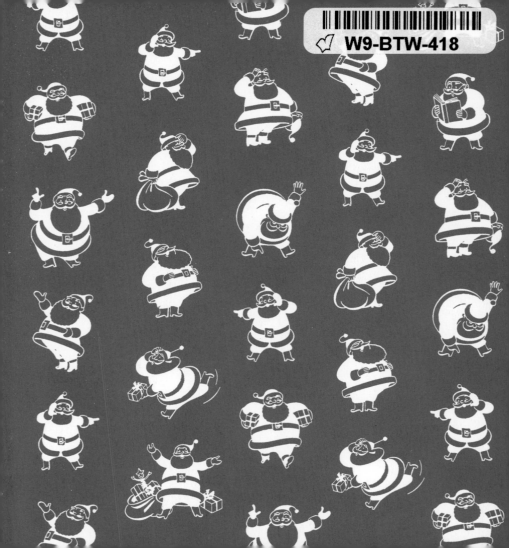

SANTA CLAUS

SANTA CLAUS

Collection of Luca Sacchi · Photographs by Franco Pizzochero

Abrams, New York

The True
Santa

Story of
Claus

Who is Santa Claus?

To millions of children the world over, Santa Claus is not only real, he is an extremely important person in their lives. It is only reluctantly that we let go of our beliefs as we enter adulthood. Yet how much do we really know about Santa Claus? Perhaps because we have grown up with such abiding affection for him—or maybe because to investigate him too closely would be to challenge his very existence—many of us are unaware of the real story behind the icon.

Many people assume that Santa Claus has been around in his present form for thousands of years. On the contrary, Santa is a modern man, born around the beginning of the nineteenth century. And the generally accepted view of Santa Claus we have today—his friendly, plump figure; the white beard and moustache below chubby,

pink cheeks; the fur-trimmed red coat and hat—
came about even later. In the mid-1800s, Thomas
Nast, a young German artist working in America,
published his first Santa illlustrations.
Nast's drawings were based on the
description of the "right jolly old
elf" found in the poem "A Visit
from St. Nicholas" (also known
as "The Night Before Christmas"), written
four decades earlier by Clement Clark Moore.

Even still, the definitive image of Santa as we
"see" him today was not generally accepted until
the 1930s when an American illustrator named
Haddon Sundblom "redesigned" Santa Claus in
the signature colors of his employer, Coca-Cola.
The corporation's annual advertising campaigns,
centered around a Coke-drinking Santa, did
much to popularize both the soft drink and the

image in our minds of a jolly, red-and-white clad man with flowing white whiskers and a sack full of presents.

Before Coca-Cola's advertising onslaught, Santa was depicted in a variety of guises and sizes. In fact, just as Santa himself, his physical image developed from a combination of beliefs and traditions. It simply took the marketing genius of one of the world's largest corporations to successfully combine and standardize them.

Santa Claus's origins can be traced back to early Christianity. And throughout the centuries—even after a complex evolutionary process of infinite transformations, concealments, migrations, and rediscoveries—he has become a part of our heritage.

Santa Claus evolved from the historical figure of Nicholas, born in Patara, in what is now Turkey, around A.D. 270. Legend has it that Nicholas's wealthy parents died when he was a boy, and he used his inheritance to help the needy and the sick. Named Bishop of Myra when he was still a young man, he quickly became known for his generous nature and his love of children. Even in his lifetime his fame spread to all corners of the world, carried by sailors who viewed the bishop as their protector.

Less than a century after his death, Nicholas was canonized as a saint in the Catholic Church. Since that time he has been widely venerated as a patron and defender of many disparate social groups, including unwed girls, children, travelers, foreigners, merchants, and even thieves. Throughout the years many stories have been told of Saint Nicholas's life and deeds and the miracles he worked. Aspects of all these accounts come together to form the modern incarnation of Santa Claus.

Saint Nicholas's generosity led to his reputation as a gift giver. In one of his most famous acts, to save three young sisters from lives of destitution, Saint Nicholas, without being seen, left sacks of money in their house. His gifts provided enough funds for dowries to secure the girls honorable weddings. Some say that he threw the sacks in through an open window, and that they landed on top of shoes and stockings left to dry by the fire. And so began the tradition of hanging stockings by the chimney.

Saint Nicholas is also known as a protector of children. He is said to have brought three youngsters, captured and killed by an evil butcher, back to life with his prayers. Another story tells of a young boy kidnapped and forced into slavery; his mother's prayers to Saint Nicholas were answered when the saint appeared to the captive boy and whisked him away, back to the safety of his mother's arms.

Saint Nicholas was also called upon in life's crucial moments of passage. In that sense he can be considered as central to the transition between the world of children and the one of grown-ups. And so it is true that the end of one's belief in Santa Claus's existence is always a passage from childhood to the adult life.

Many centuries ago, Saint Nicholas's feast day, December 6, replaced Saturnalia (a pagan celebration around the winter solstice to honor winter's power) as the most popular day for winter gift-giving. Saint Nicholas's devotees grew larger in number after 1087, when, over the objections of the Orthodox monks caring for them, his remains were removed from their obscure resting place and transferred to Bari, Italy, and placed in a splendid cathedral erected in his honor. They still rest there today.

The veneration of his sainthood continued to strengthen in the four successive centuries, until the time of the Protestant Reformation. Martin Luther's anti-papal protest expunged Nicholas and the rest of the saints from the liturgical calendar. He continued, however, to survive in the popular folklore, especially in Catholic Europe, thanks to his close ties to children and his fame for carrying gifts.

Boys in Poland and elsewhere celebrated December 6 by dressing as bishops and begging for the poor—and sometimes for themselves! In the Netherlands and Belgium, tradition had Saint Nicholas arriving on a steamship and making his gift-giving rounds riding a white horse. Observations of his feast continue to this day. For example, in Germany many children put a boot outside their door for Saint Nicholas to fill with gifts. In the Netherlands, the only mostly Protestant country where such traditions persist, Saint Nicholas's Eve is the premier day for gift-giving. Candies are thrown in the door, and

Dutch children leave carrots and hay in their shoes for his horse, hoping Nicholas will leave small presents in their place.

Nonetheless, Saint Nicholas's popularity clearly diminished after the fifteenth century, when his festival, so closely associated with the papacy, was replaced by a "Christkind" (Christ child) celebration on Christmas Eve. It was around that time that the popular figure of Father Christmas, known around the world by Weihnachtsmann, Père Noël, Babbo Natale, and other names, appeared, helping baby Jesus in the Christmas celebrations. In reality the nice little old man was a disguised Saint Nicholas, going back to older legends from pre-Christian Northern Europe as well. Soon Nicholas, baby Jesus, Father Christmas, and the rest became interchangeable figures in the Christmas observance, depending on local customs.

The big turning point in the definitive creation of Santa Claus came with the rebirth in America of a gift-carrying Saint Nicholas. The nineteenth-century Dutch immigrants that crossed the Atlantic Ocean on their way to founding New York (then New Amsterdam) brought with them not only goods to establish trading posts in the new colony but also their traditions and legends, including one that must have been the most popular—that of Saint Nicholas, protector of travelers and merchants. In America, melting pot of diverse cultures and customs, his name and celebration day settled by chance: Santa Claus evolved from the Dutch nickname for Saint Nicholas—Sinterklaas—and the date of December 25 won out over all the other days. In the beginning of the 1800s, the New York Historical Society added Santa Claus to the city's holidays calendar and in the next few years started spreading the saint's image as a dispenser of gifts standing in front of a lit fireplace—but still wearing his bishop's vestments.

On December 6, 1809, St. Nicholas's Day, the writer Washington Irving published a satiric version of New York City's Dutch beginnings. His tale, the *Knickerbocker's History of New York,* included a Dutch ship with a figurehead representing Saint Nicholas. At the entrance of the port on the night of Christmas, the figurehead came to life and took flight on a carriage pulled by horses. "Riding over the tops of the trees," he brought children gifts by descending through their chimneys. The story met with extraordinary success and was revised and enriched by Irving in 1812 and by others subsequent to him. After undergoing several variations and eventually losing any obvious religious connotations, his story finally arrived, in 1822, in Clement Clark Moore's famous poem. "A Visit from St. Nicholas" has come to define our own observations of the holiday: the stockings hung by the fireplace, the children in bed, the sleigh and reindeers, a merry little man loaded with gifts who enters each home through the chimney. Moore also bestowed upon Santa the appearance we associate with him to this day:

He was dressed all in fur,
from his head to his foot,
And his clothes were all tarnished
with ashes and soot;
[...]
His eyes—how they twinkled!
his dimples how merry!
His cheeks were like roses,
his nose like a cherry!
His droll little mouth was drawn up
like a bow,
And the beard of his chin was as white
as the snow;
The stump of a pipe
he held tight in his teeth,
And the smoke
it encircled his head like a wreath;
He had a broad face
and a little round belly,
That shook, when he laughed
like a bowlful of jelly.

The poem was conclusive. From this point on, Saint Nicholas is replaced, and Santa Claus reigns supreme. Only a dependable and unequivocal visual portrait was missing.

Such a picture was eventually supplied by Thomas Nast, who referred to the poem when he began to produce his series of drawings for *Harper's Weekly* in 1863. Here Santa Claus appeared as a sly and plump older man with a fur coat and a long white beard, carrying a bag full of toys on his shoulders. Nast's Santa in turn inspired Haddon Sundblom, the illustrator to whom we owe the ultimate, definitive transformation of Santa Claus.

Sundblom was commissioned in 1931 to conceive a new publicity campaign for

Coca-Cola. At the time, the drink was already successful in the country, but it needed an effective relaunch following a legal wrangle in which one of its product's ingredients was found to be unsuitable for children. Although the formula for Coca-Cola had changed, the company could not use children under twelve years old in its advertising. Sundblom needed to create a testimonial that could still speak to the world of childhood without alienating adults. With a stroke of genius, he chose Santa Claus, the quintessential expression of children's dreams as well as of adult nostalgia.

Sundblom wanted to depict a modern Santa, one that was both more realistic and more familiar. To achieve his goal, he used as his model one of his neighbors, an ordinary man, stout and pleasant, with a cheerful, reassuring face. Sundblom simply rounded off his subject's waistline, colored his puffy cheeks with red, and dressed him in a red coat and hat with white trim. The resulting image was an incredible triumph both in terms of the drink's sales and in the myth's diffusion throughout the world. Thanks to the Coca-Cola publicity, Santa Claus crossed back over the Atlantic and progressively conquered the Old World and all the countries invaded by the Atlanta firm.

Sundblom's illustrations did much to cement a single, lovable image of Santa Claus in our minds, but the Santa myth itself gained such immense success because it offered a world suspended between reality and imagination.

Santa Claus gives joy to even the youngest of children while he allows adults to travel back to their otherwise lost world of childhood. Every year he makes us rediscover—in case we have forgotten—the positive values of generosity and good will. His appeal is such that it transcends differences of ethnicity, social class, skin color, and sometimes even religious beliefs.

Our collective passion for Santa Claus therefore is not surprising. It is an excitement that is renewed in each of us, and not only when the holiday season approaches. How many Santa Clauses spark our memories? The simple sight of a Santa figure, whether familiar or unusual, can be enough to bring back a treasured Christmas moment from our past, long thought to be forgotten.

Luca Sacchi has a special, collector's passion for all things Santa. With attention and dedication, he has held on to all his Santa Clauses from the past while he continues to build his collection with pieces from every part of the world. By searching, pursuing, and chasing down precious items and modest ones, traditional and unique, antique and contemporary,

small and monumental, he has assembled an
immense and magnificent collection of Santa
Clauses. Some of his pieces are functional,
others decorative; some are the fruit of
an artisan's painstaking craftsmanship,
others creations of industrial manu-
facturers. Whatever their origin,
and whatever their purpose, the
variety of Santa Claus's representation
in his collection finds a counterpoint in the
inexhaustible fantasy of the human mind that,
when allowed to turn childlike, knows neither
limits nor borders.

Here comes…

Santa Claus

Christmas tree ornament, plastic, 1998

Figurine, stamped card, around 1920. German production, purchased in Connecticut.

nin

ring ring

ring ring

ring

ring

"Merry Olde Santa," Christmas tree ornament, 1993. Hallmark

Landing in American ports
with the Dutch, Sinterklaas, a
gift-carrying Saint Nicholas,
was transformed at the turn
of the nineteenth century
into Santa Claus.

Jingle bells,

jingle bells,

jingle all the way!

Sticker, 1988. Purchased in New York. The eyes move as in an animated card.

Lamp in Bakelite/hard plastic, 1960. Purchased at a flea market in New York City.

In 1822 Clement Clark Moore
wrote a poem for children that for
the first time described Saint
Nicholas as a jolly old man
who drives a sleigh pulled by
eight reindeer, and who slides
down chimneys to bring gifts to
children on the night of
Christmas.

In the second half of the 1900s, the most famous American illustrator of his time, Thomas Nast, created drawings that defined the image of Santa Claus that we all know and love today.

Christmas tree ornament, Celluloid, around 1920–30. Japan

Santa Claus's red costume and new residence at the North Pole were the creations of Thomas Nast.

Figurine, crayon tempera. China

Christmas tree ornament, metal, 2004. Upper right: ceramic, 1998

Christmas tree ornament, resin, 2003

How to recognize Santa:

WEARS A FUNNY RED HAT
WITH A WHITE POM-POM

HAS A WHITE BEARD,
A MOUSTACHE,
AND A RED NOSE

SMELLS LIKE
WARM COOKIES

BELLS RING WHEN
HE ARRIVES

"Jolly Visitor," Christmas tree ornament, 1994. Hallmark

Luca Sacchi's first box of Santas, 1989

Super
Santa!

Saltshaker, 1950. United States, Chinese production

Ho, ho, ho!

Red jacket with white furry
borders and a big black belt;
Red hat underlined with a smile
inside a soft white beard;
Red pants and big black boots

the big black boots...

...and the snowshoes!

Christmas tree ornament, stamped card, Germany

From the movie *Rudolf, the Red-Nosed Reindeer*, 2004

Merry Christmas!

Make him move by pressing your thumb under the base

snowflakes

In 1931 the illustrator and publicist
Haddon Sundblom created
the official drawing of
Santa Claus for Coca-Cola
…an icon of "modern" Christmas.

Cheers!

...What a Christmas!

"Relaxed moment," Coca-Cola Santa, 1994. Hallmark

Figurine, colored cast iron, 1938. Purchased at the Columbus Avenue market, New York City.

A friend to all,
Santa Claus never
forgets anyone.

How does Santa Claus work?

Even Santa Claus needs some
basic equipment for his work:
reindeer and sled to travel,
a bag to carry the gifts, and
chimneys to get into the houses.

The moon on the breast of the new-fallen snow

Gave the lustre of mid-day to objects below,

When, what to my wondering eyes should appear,

But a miniature sleigh, and eight tiny reindeer

[...]

FROM "A VISIT FROM ST. NICHOLAS" BY CLEMENT C. MOORE

Santa Claus is is coming to town!

Figurine, lead, United States, 1991

coming...

With a little old driver, so lively and quick,

I knew in a moment it must be Saint Nick.

More rapid than eagles his coursers they came,

And he whistled, and shouted, and called them by name

[...]

FROM "A VISIT FROM ST. NICHOLAS" BY CLEMENT C. MOORE

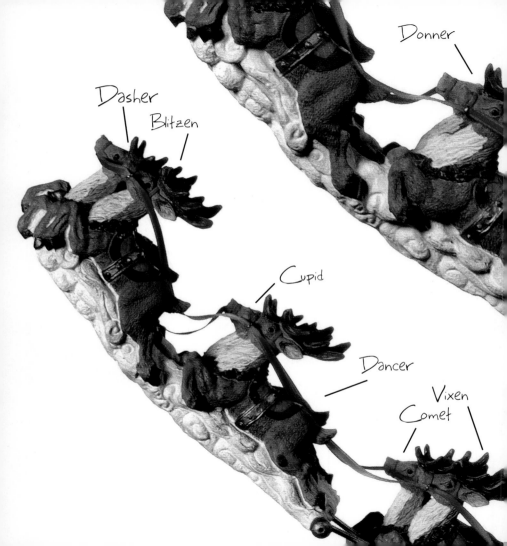

Prancer

on Dasher!
on Comet!

"Kris and the Kringles #3," 2003. Hallmark.

The campfire flickers!

pa'rum

pum pum

pum

ring ring

toot-toot

Dashing through the snow
In a one-horse open sleigh,
O'er the fields we go,
Laughing all the way
Bells on bob-tail ring
Making spirits bright
Oh, what fun it is to ride and sing
A sleighing song tonight.
Oh, jingle bells, jingle bells,
Jingle all the way.

Oh, what fun it is to ride
In a one-horse open sleigh

He sprang to his sleigh,

to his team gave a whistle,

And away they all flew

like the down of a thistle.

But I heard him exclaim,

'ere he drove out of sight,

"Happy Christmas to all,

and to all a good-night!"

FROM "A VISIT FROM ST. NICHOLAS" BY CLEMENT C. MOORE

Bon Marché, 2005. Left Bank, Paris

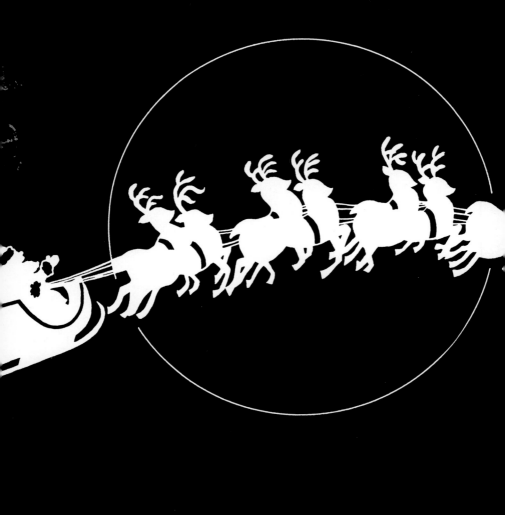

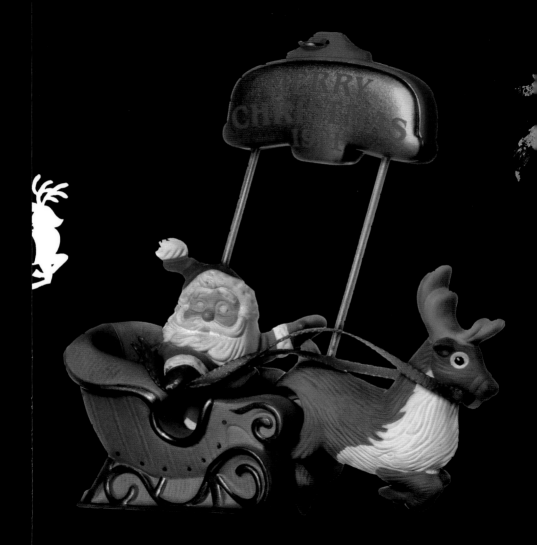

Music box

The reindeer and sled
fly over a small village.

ON
Blitzen!

Everything moves with the music.

Hallmark Magic

Celluloid lamp, 1960. United States

The trip from
the North Pole
is very long...
the secret
is to face it
with cheer!

Santa and his reindeer run
around the North Pole. "North Pole Merrython," 1993. Hallmark

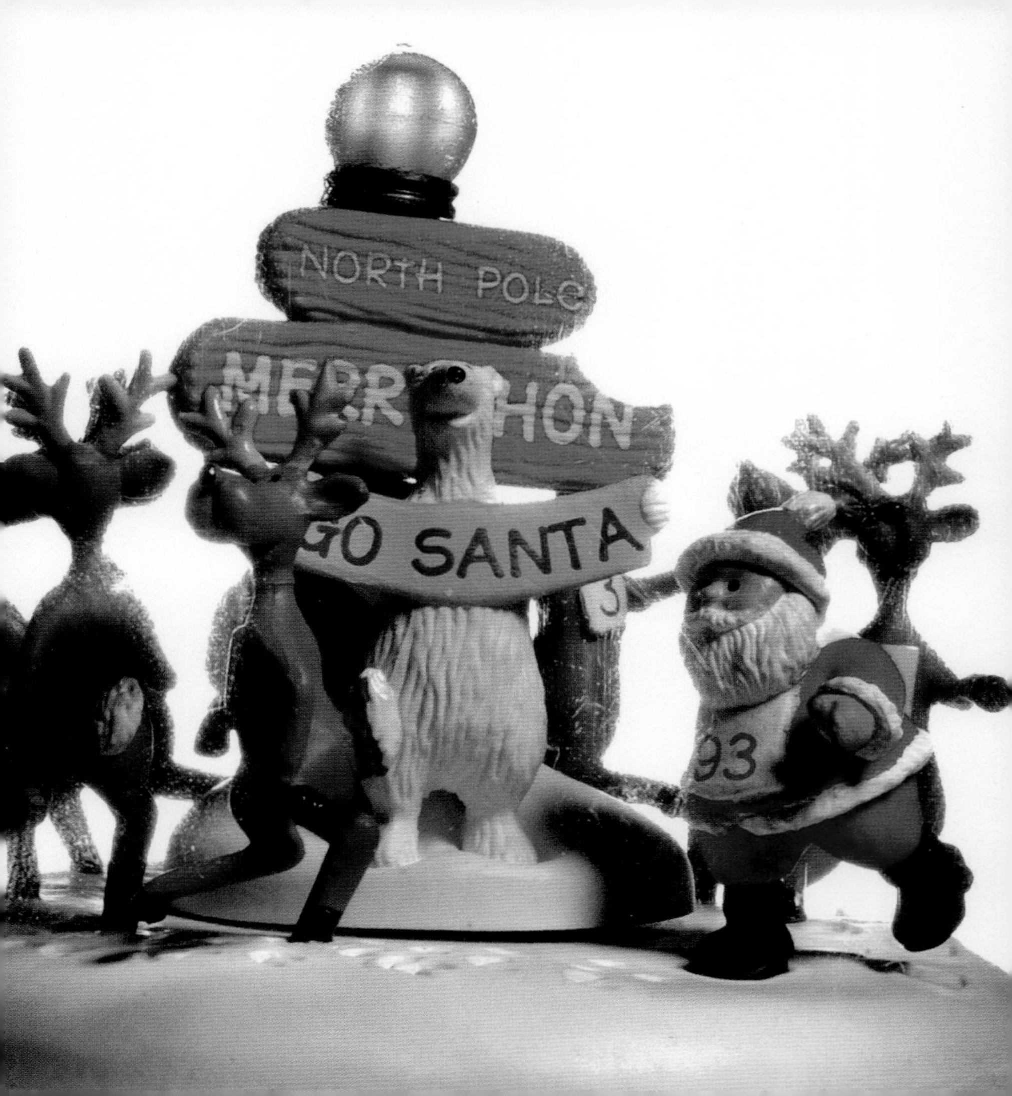
NORTH POLE
GO SANTA
93

Clippety

clop

*Now, **Dasher!** now, **Dancer!***

*now, **Prancer** and **Vixen!***

*On, **Comet!** on **Cupid!***

*on, **Donder** and **Blitzen!***

FROM "A VISIT FROM ST. NICHOLAS" BY CLEMENT C. MOORE

Ceramic candleholder, around 1940–50. Produced in Japan, purchased in New York.

what
happened
to the
reindeer?

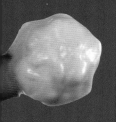

So up to the house-top the coursers they flew,

With the sleigh full of toys, and

Saint Nicholas *too.*

And then, in a twinkling, I heard on the roof

The prancing and pawing of each little hoof.

FROM "A VISIT FROM ST. NICHOLAS" BY CLEMENT C. MOORE

"Down the chimney Saint Nicholas...

...came with a bound."

The bigger
the chimney,
the more gifts
will fit!

shhhhh...

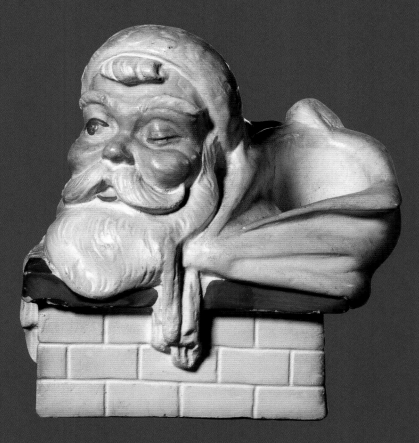

Figurine, ceramic, 1950. United States. Purchased at a flea market in New York City.

the lights can be turned on!!

1 inch

3/4 inch

1 1/4 inch

This is a brooch! Santa Claus's head moves,
and so do the stockings.
Purchased in New York in 1999

Nobody knows
exactly how large
Santa Claus's
gift bag is…

How heavy are these gifts?

Plastic brooch, 1999

Christmas tree decoration, plastic, 1995

shhhhh...

Plastic bank, 1970. United States

All in plastic, 1965. United States

"Santa's Magic Sack," Christmas tree ornament, 2005. Hallmark

"Santa's Magic Sack," Christmas tree ornament, 2005. Hallmark

Surely his bag
must be able to
hold a lot of
gifts…

Resin, 1997

Covered light bulb, part of a twelve-light set

How much does
Santa's bag weigh?
It never gets
empty...

Miniature ornament (1³⁄₈ inches high), 1995. Hallmark

Miniature ornament (1³/₈ inches high), 1998. Hallmark

Celluloid lamp, 1960. United States

Salt-and-pepper shakers, ceramic, 1992.

Figurines, wood, 1999

Carved by a dreamer.

What are inside these beautifully decorated packages?
Toys, wishes, dreams, and hopes.

a very

special

present

for you!

Santa

Candleholder, stained glass with lead, 1995

Just
for you!

Cooking for
Santa Claus

Santa Claus's frenetic activity requires remarkable energy. To help fuel his yearly journey, he relies on snacks left out for him all over the world. Here are some recipes for delicious sweets and energizing drinks. Of course serve them with a theme…

Chocolate Chip Cookies

½ cup unsalted butter, room
   temperature
½ cup light brown sugar
¼ cup white granulated sugar
1 large egg
1 teaspoon pure vanilla extract
1 cup all-purpose flour

¼ cup Dutch-processed cocoa
   powder
½ teaspoon baking soda
⅛ teaspoon salt
1½ cups chocolate chips (white,
   dark, or milk chocolate chips)

- Preheat oven to 350 degrees F and place rack in center of oven. Line two
  baking sheets with parchment paper.
- In bowl of electric mixer, fitted with the paddle attachment, cream the
  butter and sugars until light and fluffy (2–3 minutes). Add the egg and
  vanilla extract and beat until incorporated.
- First sift together the cocoa powder, flour, baking soda, and salt, and
  then add to the butter and egg mixture. Mix just until incorporated.
  Fold in the chocolate chips.
- Form dough into 1 inch balls and arrange on the prepared baking sheet
  about 2 inches apart.
- Bake for approximately 8 minutes or until the cookies are still soft in the
  center but are firm around the edges. Remove from oven and let
  cookies cool on baking sheet for about 5 minutes before removing the
  cookies to a wire rack to cool completely.

Makes about 40 2-inch cookies.

Note: Can also use a combination of chocolate chips, toffee bits, and even toasted nuts.

a snack
for the trip

♡ ♡

1 *chocolate chip* **COOKIE**	=	104 calories
1 *chocolate chip* **COOKIE**	=	1 WEIGHT WATCHERS point
1 *chocolate chip* **COOKIE**	=	guaranteed happiness

"Sweet Tooth treats #2," Christmas tree ornament, 2003. Hallmark

Cookie jar lid opens

gingerbread men

ginger b read man

Santa loves cookies

Cookie-cutter, 1940. United States. Purchased at a flea market in New York, 1995

...a cookie and a

kiss under the mistletoe...

That's Christmas magic.

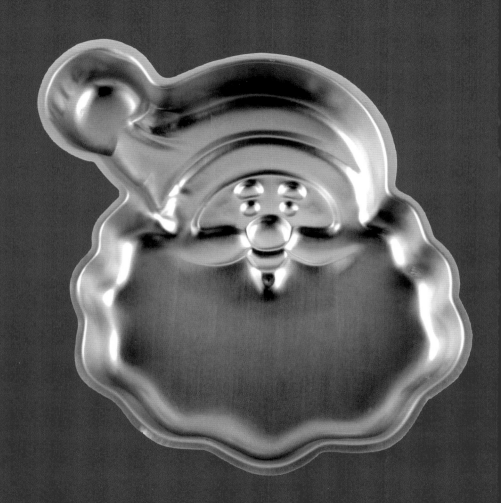

Gingerbread Men

3 cups all-purpose flour
¼ teaspoon salt
¾ teaspoon baking soda
2 teaspoons ground ginger
1 teaspoon ground cinnamon
¼ teaspoon ground nutmeg
¼ teaspoon ground cloves
½ cup unsalted butter, room
    temperature
½ cup granulated white sugar
1 large egg
⅔ cup (160 ml) unsulphured molasses

Note: To prevent the molasses from sticking to
the measuring cup, first spray the cup
with a nonstick vegetable spray (like Pam).

ROYAL ICING USING MERINGUE POWDER:
1½ tablespoons meringue powder
2 cups confectioners sugar
    (powdered or icing)
3–4 tablespoons warm water
¼ teaspoon pure orange extract
    (optional)
Makes about 1½ cups

Note: Meringue powder is a fine,
white powder used to replace fresh egg
whites in royal icing. You can purchase
meringue powder in most cake decorating
and party stores.

- In a large bowl, sift or whisk together the flour, salt, baking soda, and spices. Set aside. In the bowl of your electric mixer, with the paddle attachment, cream the butter and sugar until light and fluffy. Add the egg and molasses and beat until well combined. Gradually add the flour mixture beating until incorporated. Divide the dough in half, and wrap each half in plastic wrap and refrigerate for at least two hours or overnight.
- Preheat oven to 350 degrees F and place rack in center of oven. Line 2 baking sheets with parchment paper and set aside while you roll out the dough.

[TURN PAGE]

- On a lightly floured surface, roll out the dough to a thickness of about ⅛–¼ inch. Use a gingerbread cutter to cut out the cookies. With an offset spatula lift the cut-out cookies onto the baking sheet, placing the cookies about 1 inch apart. If you are hanging the cookies or using as gift tags, make a hole at the top of the cookies with a straw or end of a wooden skewer. Bake for about 8–12 minutes depending on the size of the cookies. Smaller cookies will take about 8 minutes, larger cookies will take about 12 minutes. They are done when they are firm and the edges are just beginning to brown.
- Remove the cookies from the oven and cool on the baking sheet for about 1 minute. When they are firm enough to move, transfer to a wire rack to cool completely. If desired, you can press raisins, currants, or candies into the dough for eyes and buttons while the cookies are still warm. Otherwise, royal icing can be used to decorate the cookies. You can also use the royal icing as a glue to attach candies, raisins, and sprinkles.

To make the Royal Icing:
- In the bowl of your electric mixer, with the whisk attachment, place the meringue powder, confectioners sugar, and water. Beat at low speed until the sugar is moistened. Increase the speed to high and beat for about 5–7 minutes or until very glossy and stiff peaks form. Beat in the orange extract, if using. Add more water or sugar as necessary to get the right consistency for piping. Transfer to a piping bag and decorate as desired.
- Makes about 3 dozen cookies depending on the size of cookie cutter used. Store in an airtight container for several weeks.

Cookie cutter, clear plastic, 1997. United States

Lollipop mold, 1998. Germany

To be eaten on
Christmas Day

Bittersweet, milk, and white chocolates.

Box, metal, 1930. Germany

Alemagna box, metal, 1960. Italy

Stacking food containers, 2004

Giddy up, Comet!

Here comes Santa Claus

who
wants
a cookie???

Ceramic cookie jar, 1993. 17 3/8 inches high

Sweets tray, 2005

Papier-mâché box, 1994

Cookie jar, plastic, around 1950–60. United States

Christmas Tea

This is my recipe for a delicious hot punch for the holidays. To make it more festive, you can float orange rings in the punch.

Santa Claus

2 cups granulated sugar
1½ quarts water
3 oranges, juice of
1 lemon, juice of
4 ounces red cinnamon candies
   (otherwise known as cinnamon imperials)
20 ounces pineapple juice (1 can)
2 quarts cranberry juice

Makes approximately 4 quarts
25 minutes to make with 5 minutes prep

Would you like more Christmas Tea?

Ceramic teapot, 1997

Nothing is better than a cup of good hot tea before leaving for the long Christmas night. Isn't that right, Donder?

Sugar bowl, ceramic, around 1960–70. United States. Produced in China.

GLOGG
Swedish Christmas Punch

Glogg means glow. The name is derived from the burning of the sugar over the drink. It is the most common Swedish Christmas punch bowl drink and is also well liked by many Danes and Finns. Nowadays *glogg* is often served less strong than in the recipe below. It is often made exclusively of dry red wine, aquavit being omitted. Ready-mixed *glogg* spices are sold in many Scandinavian delicatessen stores.

1 bottle Burgundy, Claret, or other dry red wine	4 dried figs
10 cardamom seeds	1½ inch cinnamon stick
5 whole cloves	1 cup raisins
3 pieces dried orange peel	½ pound sugar cubes
	1 cup blanched almonds

Pour liquor and wine into kettle. Add remaining ingredients except sugar cubes. Cover and heat slowly to boiling point. Remove from heat. Put sugar in sieve with long handle. Dip into hot liquid to moisten. Light sugar with a match and allow to burn. Continue dipping sieve into liquid until sugar has melted into *glogg*. Cover kettle to put out flame. Put through sieve. Cool. Keep in closed bottles.

Heat *glogg* before serving, but do not boil. Serve hot in wine glasses with a few raisins and almonds in each glass.

Milk jug, 1980. England

Christmas Punch

(traditional recipe)

2 pints water
8 ounces sugar
juice and rind of 3 lemons
half a bottle rum
half a bottle port
grated nutmeg
1 apple sliced
1 orange sliced

Boil the water, sugar, and lemon
rind in a saucepan. Allow to cool
a little and strain. Add the rum,
port, and lemon juice. Transfer
into a pre-warmed large bowl.
Float the fruit on top
and sprinkle with nutmeg.

Christmas Eve Punch

(nonalcoholic)

1 (32 ounces) bottle cranberry juice
1 (46 ounces) can unsweetened
   pineapple juice
2 cups orange juice
½ cup sugar
2 teaspoons almond extract
1 (32 ounces) ginger ale

Combine first 6 ingredients.
Chill to serve. Add ginger ale.
Makes 4½ quarts

*Time is
running out
I have to run!!*

ticktock

*ticktock
ticktock*

ticktock

Santa Claus arrives in the
Sacchi house somewhere
around December 1.

ticktock

ticktock

ticktock

In the kitchen...
Santa-shaped corks,
silverware, bottle openers,
timers...

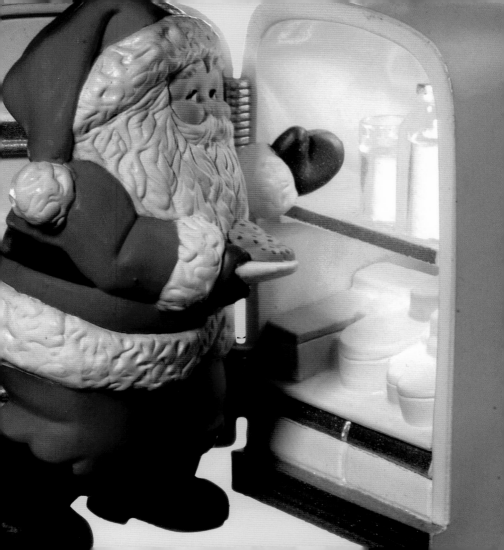

Carving knife
and fork
for Christmas
dinner

Bottle opener and butter knife, 1999

In the bathroom...
The soap dish,
the toothbrush,
the toilet tissue,
the fragrance
bottle...

Liquid-soap dispenser, 1996. New York

Clothespin for Santa's laundry!
Mrs. Claus uses it to hang his
socks, undershirt, pants, jacket,
and hat...

on

Is anybody there?

It's completely dark in here.

CUT HERE

CUT HERE   CUT HERE

CUT HERE

I'm comiiingggg...

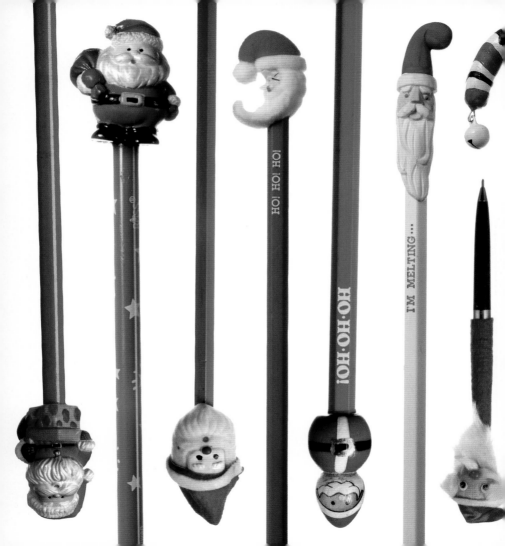

Pencils and pens to write letters to Santa!

HO HO HO!

China

APPLAUSE ™ 1988 TAIWAN

Dear
Santa Claus

Letters addressed to Santa Claus express the dreams, hopes, and desires of children, who also write about their best intentions and promises for the next year. Santa is generous and always willing to believe them.

To make sure you receive a gift from
Santa Claus, it is recommended that
you write him a nice letter...
and send it to the exact address:

Santa Claus
Arctic Polar Circle
96930 Rovaniemi
Finland

Sometimes he answers...

...but even if he doesn't,
he always fulfills our wishes—
if they are not too ambitious!

Baby's First Christmas
1991

Dear Santa Claus,

Dear Santa Claus,
Again this year I was very
good. Don't listen to what
my sister says about her
doll and most of all
don't pay attention
to what Mom and
Dad say about
me— they're all
lies. I would like...

...led, and a wagon, and a book, a

Santa,
I would like...
...and also...

if there is
room on
your sled
for...

really I have
been so
good that...

The magic of Christmas Eve
inspires peace and joy
in everyone's heart.
It really is the most
extraordinary night
of the year!

Everybody come together for a beautiful
souvenir picture with Santa Claus!

Say, "Santa"...

flash
flash!

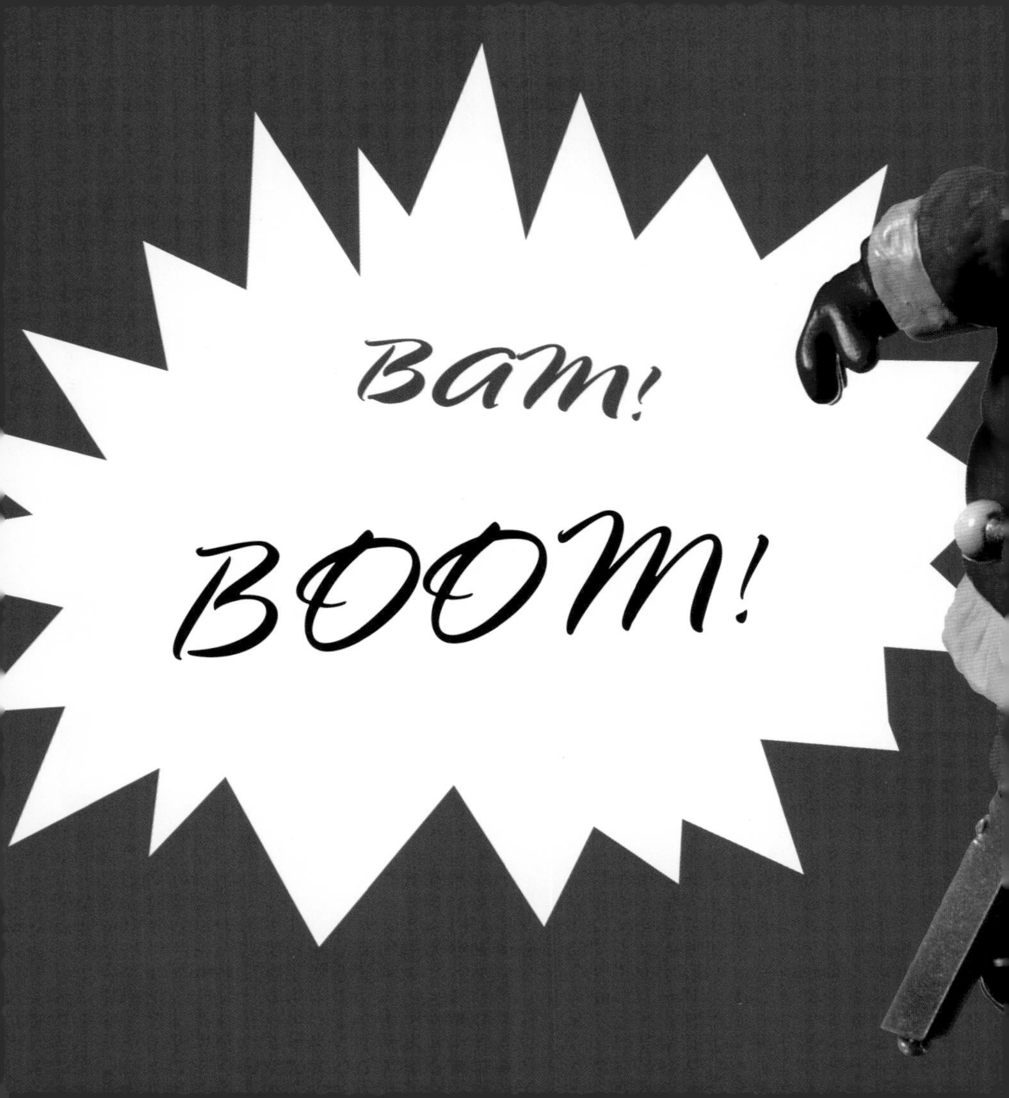
Bam!
BOOM!

wee !!

*oops...
I fell...*

Santa Claus is a
perfect playmate…
always smiling
and always there
for you.

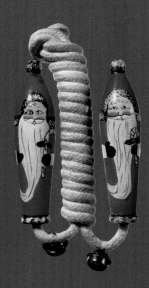

On Christmas... NO STRESS

swoosh

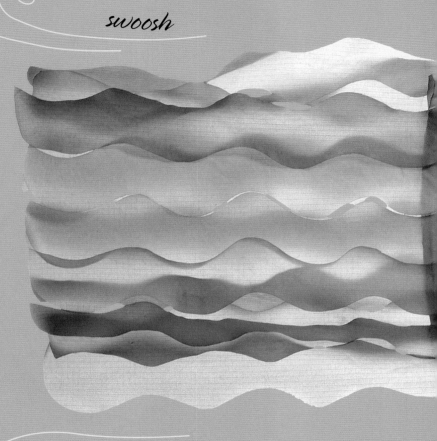

swooshhh

Windsock. Purchased in the United States

A rubber stamp with Santa's face

Even Lego® thought of Santa Claus. December 2005

tweeeet!

Nothing works better than a whistle to call the reindeer.

sparkle

sparkle

a
spinning Santa...

Tin yo-yo, 2001. Purchased in New York

Spinning top, 1960. United States

Hooray for
Santa!

Hooray!! Hooray!

Jingle Bells, Jingle Bells,

Jingle all the way!

Oh what fun it is to ride

In a one-horse open sleigh.

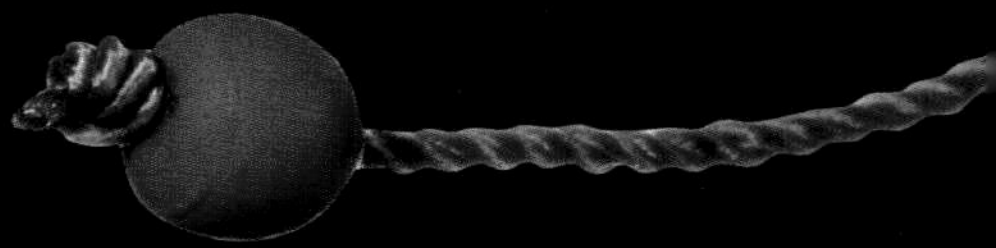

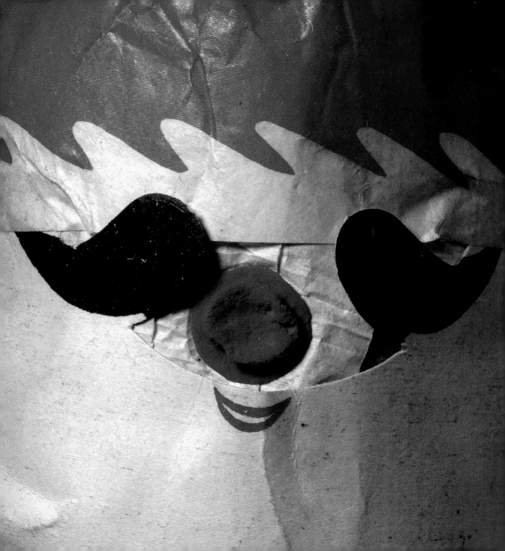

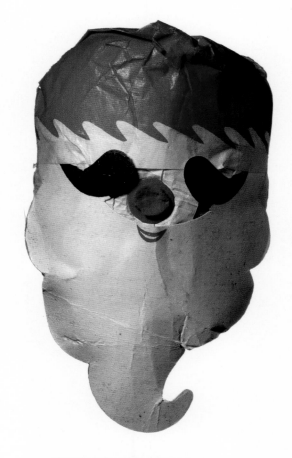

"Surprise ball," cardboard, 1946. Japan.

There is a little surprise inside...do not open until Christmas!

Mr. and Mrs. Santa Claus

Santa Claus has a wife, Mrs. Claus, who helps Santa and the elves in the North Pole.

Mrs. Claus is a very loving wife.

kiss!
kiss!

May I present my wife,
Mrs. Claus!

Even more than the elves,
she is Santa's favorite helper.

Santa, don't
forget to...

1980. United States

Salt-and-pepper shakers, 1970. United States

Christmas
Is
Love

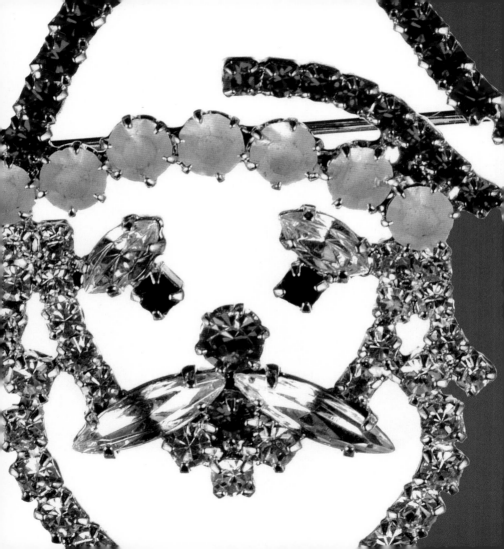

Clearly Mrs. Claus adores her husband. Even her jewelry is in his likeness!

Cameo (costume jewelry), 1960. United States

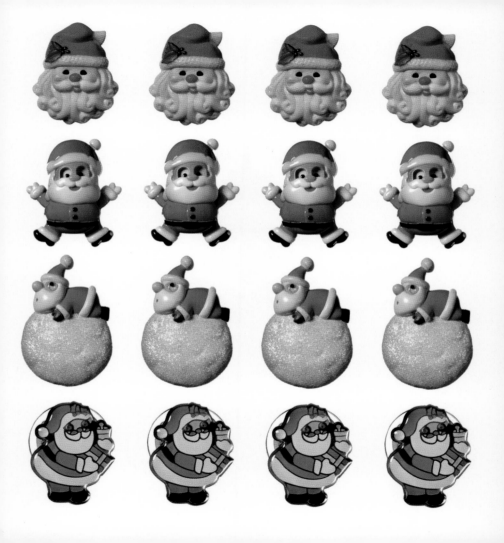

Mrs. Claus's jewelry are gifts from Santa.

Pendant (costume Jewelry), 1960. United States

Costume jewelry, 1960. United States

Ring once
for
each good child.

ticktock ticktock ticktock

On the
road on
Christmas Eve

Santa Claus is an extraordinary traveler. He covers the entire world in one night, and he's never once been late, even if circumstance demands he leaves the sleigh at home.

Where do I finish??

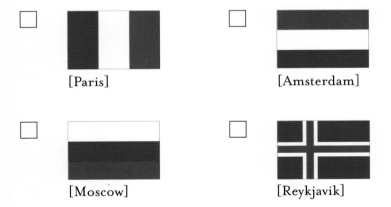

☐ [Paris]

☐ [Amsterdam]

☐ [Moscow]

☐ [Reykjavik]

[THE SOLUTION IS ON THE FOLLOWING SPREAD.]

Santa Claus has been seen
in Venice, in Paris,
in New York…

Glass, Venice. 2004

Glass, Venice. 2004

...and also at the
window of
your bedroom!

Santa Claus around the world

In Great Britain, *Father Christmas* arrives on the back of a goat or a white donkey wearing a crown made of holly and ivy.

In Russia, *Grandfather Frost* wears a blue uniform instead of the traditional red outfit.

In The Netherlands, *Sinterklaes* traditionally arrives on a ship on December 6th and then travels on land with gifts riding a white horse.

In Finland, *Joulupukki* does not come down chimneys but enters through the main door to personally deliver presents.

In Korea, *Santa Claus* wears a tall hat and carries the gifts on his back in a large wicker basket.

In Japan, an old man called *Santa Kurousu* travels by foot and delivers gifts that he hauls in a bag on his back. He also has eyes on the back of his neck to spy on children's behavior.

In Mexico, *Santa* is present when the children break a hanging terra-cotta pineapple filled with sweets.

In China, Christians hang their stockings for *Che Dun Lao Ren* (the elderly man of Christmas) and *Lan Khoong* (the nice old father).

choo choo

There are not only reindeer!!!
Santa Claus drives a car and a truck…
an airplane and a balloon…
he is the train conductor and he flies
on a tricycle…
…this is only possible during the
magical night of Christmas!

blurp

blurp

USS PEPPERMINT

Even the little fish and other creatures of the sea receive gifts on Christmas...
but the reindeer cannot swim...

chimney in sight!

SPECIAL DELIVERY

KRINGLE & CO.

Who knows
where we are?
It's too dark
to see anything!

In some places it is warm
and there is no snow
on Christmas…
that's why Santa Claus
brings delicious ice
cream from the
North Pole!

Metal and plastic, 1960. United States

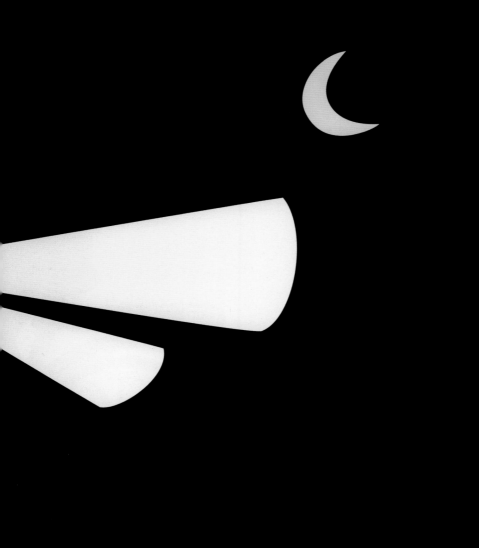

REYKJAVIK

RDAM

PARIS

The Santamobile

STANDARD HEADLIGHTS,
IDEAL FOR NIGHT VISIBILITY

PERSONALIZED
LICENSE PLATE

ATMOSPHERIC TIRES,
RESISTANT TO FRICTION
WITH CHRISTMAS AIR
[WARRANTY: 2 CENTURIES]

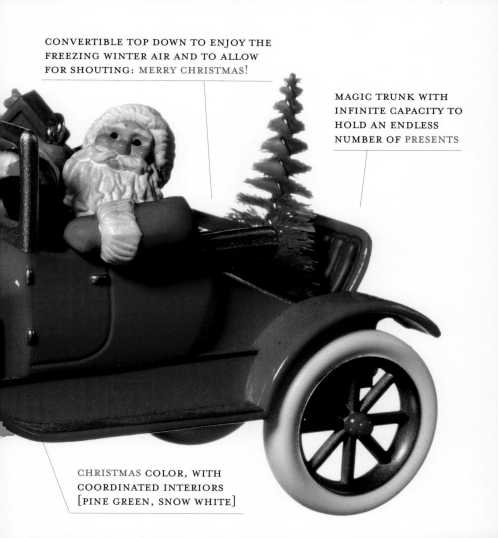

CONVERTIBLE TOP DOWN TO ENJOY THE
FREEZING WINTER AIR AND TO ALLOW
FOR SHOUTING: MERRY CHRISTMAS!

MAGIC TRUNK WITH
INFINITE CAPACITY TO
HOLD AN ENDLESS
NUMBER OF PRESENTS

CHRISTMAS COLOR, WITH
COORDINATED INTERIORS
[PINE GREEN, SNOW WHITE]

At last,
we're here!!

The trip is always more
fun with friends along.
Let's all sing together:

Jingle Bells, jingle bells,
jingle all the way...

Too many gifts??
Santa has a
solution!

LS 25

Thoroughly Modern Santa!

When it comes to updating his image, there is no limit to the creativity Santa Claus has shown... He's always in step with the times. His tale, however, remains intact...

Like most modern men, Santa knows how important exercise is to health. To make sure he's in shape for the magical night, Santa Claus does gymnastics and aerobics, he jumps and dances…

one

two

three

Kick!

His cheeks
become even
more rosy

a few
   sit-ups...

And
he's
ready
to go
around
the
world!!

He's making a list,
and checking it twice;
gonna find out who's naughty and nice.
Santa Claus is coming to town

He sees you when you're sleeping
he knows when you're awake
he knows if you've been bad or good
so be good for goodness sake!

Santa Claus's costume can also change. He's certainly no stranger to high-fashion outfits, fancy materials, and colors. Sometimes he can appear trendy, thin, or more colorful, with his hat stretched or squashed....
That's the magic of Santa!

Celluloid bank, 1950. United States

Santa's hat is
sooo long
    it doesn't even
fit on the page!

Here's a star-capped
Santa Claus at the guitar
and Mr. Snowman at
percussions!

long arms

long arms

long legs long legs long legs

long legs long legs long legs long legs

long legs long legs long legs

very very very very tall!!!

TREE MADE FROM
LEFTOVERS FROM
SANTA'S WORKSHOP

TRIANGULAR BUTTONS
[SUGGESTING THE
CHRISTMAS TREE SHAPE]

BLUE GLOVES
WITH PASTEL
FLOWER DESIGNS

RED PANTS, SLIM FIT,
BOOTLEG, WITH
GLITTERY FINISH

WARM AND VERY TRENDY
BLACK BOOTS, WITH
STUDS AND LACES

EXTRA-LONG HAT, LACKING
A REAL FUNCTION BUT
INCREDIBLY GLAMOROUS

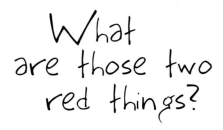

What are those two red things?

☐ An extraterrestrial's antenna

☐ Santa Claus's drumstick

☐ Chopsticks to eat sushi

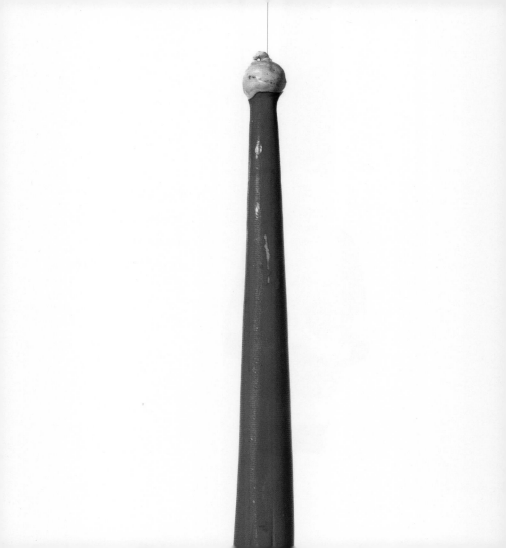

Wrong!
The correct answer is...

☐ The top of
Santa Claus's hat
made into two
dangling earrings

Lots of glitter makes this Christmas outfit especially festive. A little jingle on the cap and red curling shoes don't hurt, either!

Lead, 1992. France

We are made of tin!

But what material are those made of?

Fluorescent colors for a
Christmas filled with light!

Ho, ho, ho!

Elements
of style

CHRISTMAS HOLLY
[MOVES IN RHYTHM
WITH THE MUSIC]

MOTHER-OF-PEARL
DECORATIONS GIVE
MAGIC SPARKS

RED OVERCOAT
EMBELLISHED WITH
NEVER-MELTING
SNOWFLAKES

RED ANKLE BOOTS
WITH SPANGLES

snow effect

WHITE

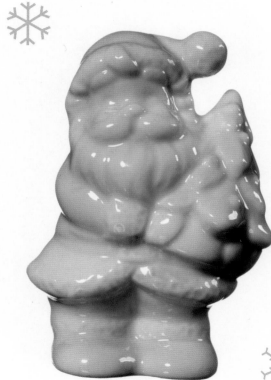

Music box, ceramic, 1980. United States

Polyester/paper/glitter handmade product, 1960. Made in a New York school

Figurine, ceramic, 1970. United States

oh what a joy

every snowflake brings!

Santa number 100, 1991. New York

Merry
Christmas!

All around the world
there are many ways to
offer Christmas greetings.

Fröliche Weihnachten!

would be what a
German would say,

and a Hawaiian would
certainly reply with a friendly

Mele Kalikimaka!

Feliz
Navidad!

In Greek, it's

Kala Christougena!

While a Swede would
joyfully shout

God Yul!

God Yul!

Happy
Christmas!

is what they say in
the United Kingdom

Melkm Ganna!

is the Ethiopians'
Merry Christmas...

and if you find yourself in the

Philippines you will hear the greeting

Maligayang Pasko!

In France they say *Joyeux Noël!*

In Italy *Buon Natale!*

And once you return home from the trip around the world you can happily wish everyone a Merry Christmas!

LUCA SACCHI
COLLECTION
AND CREATION

FRANCO PIZZOCHERO
PHOTOGRAPHY

LAURA MAGGIONI
EDITORIAL
COORDINATION
AND IDEA

Santa Claus's helpers

those who participated in the creation of the
creation of this book

PAOLA FAVRETTO
TEXTS

VIRGINIA MACCAGNO
PROJECT DESIGN
AND IDEA

Santa Claus and the publisher would like to thank Franco Pizzochero and Luca Sacchi for their amusing initiative and for making the Christmas spirit last all year round.

Translated from the Italian by *Magali Veillon*

Project Manager, English-language edition: *Jon Cipriaso*
Copyeditor, English-language edition: *Beverly Herter*
Designer, English-language edition: *Shawn Dahl*
Production Manager, English-language edition: *Colin Hough Trapp*

Library of Congress Control Number:
2006930147
ISBN 10: 0-8109-3089-7
ISBN 13: 978-0-8109-3089-6

Originally published under the title *Babbo Natale: vita, renne e misteri*

Copyright © 2006 by Equatore srl, Milan
English translation © 2006 Abrams, New York

The objects represented in this book belong to the collection of Luca Sacchi.

Photograph separations: Eurofotolit, Cernusco sul Naviglio, Milan, Italy

Printed and bound in Italy
10 9 8 7 6 5 4 3 2 1

HNA ■■■■■
harry n. abrams, inc.
a subsidiary of La Martinière Groupe
115 West 18th Street
New York, NY 10011
www.hnabooks.com